So Man Questions

How to answer 17 common questions about Christianity

by Simon Roberts and Tony Payne

Let your conversation be always full of grace, seasoned with salt, so that you may know how to answer everyone. (Col 4:6)

So Many Questions
© Matthias Media, 2001.

Distributed in the U.K. by
The Good Book Company
Elm House
37 Elm Road, New Malden
Surrey KT3 3HB
Tel: (020) 8942 0880
Fax: (020) 8942-0990
Email: admin@thegoodbook.co.uk

ISBN 1 876326 35 2

Cover design and typesetting by Joy Lankshear Design Pty Ltd

Contents

About this course 5

Introduction: How to answer questions 9

The 17 questions

  1. How do I know God exists in the first place? 13

  2. Is the New Testament story about Jesus reliable? 15

  3. Wasn't Jesus just another great religious teacher? 17

  4. Did Jesus really come back from the dead? 19

  5. Hasn't science disproved Christianity? 21

  6. How do we account for all the suffering in the world? 23

  7. Does 'faith' mean believing things we can't accept? 25

  8. What about miracles—can miracles actually happen? 27

  9. What about those people who have never heard about Jesus? 29

  10. What about other religions: are they all true? 31

  11. Aren't all people basically good? 33

  12. Can we just be good enough to please God? 35

  13. Do you have to go to church to be a Christian? 37

  14. Could it be said that the Bible is sexist? 39

  15. What does the Bible say about homosexuality? 41

  16. Isn't Christianity responsible for a great deal of the 43
      environmental disaster in our world?

  17. Aren't Christians just hypocrites? 45

Where to from here? 47

About this course

Welcome to *So Many Questions*, a video-based training course in how to answer common questions about Christianity. By using this workbook, and the accompanying video, trainees will learn some general principles for answering people's questions, as well as the specifics of how to answer 17 frequently asked questions.

There are 18 units in the course: an introduction, plus the 17 questions, with each unit designed to last about 20 minutes. The basic format of each unit is simple:

   a. The trainee tries to work out briefly how he or she would answer the question based on their current knowledge; if the course is done in a group this could be briefly discussed.

   b. The trainee then watches the relevant short segment of video, taking notes in the space provided.

   c. The trainee then writes down a final summary of the main points he or she would use in answering the question.

Different ways to use the course

With each unit being quite brief, there is considerable flexibility in how the course might be used. Here are some suggestions:

- An individual or couple could work through one unit per week (say each Friday night or Sunday afternoon) as part of their personal Christian growth.
- A small Bible study group could do one unit each week during their regular meeting together (taking just 15-20 minutes each week).
- The units could be grouped together to yield more intensive courses of different lengths; a nine-week course (two at a time = 40 minutes); or even a six-week course (three at a time = 60 minutes).
- Group leaders/co-ordinators could also choose not to cover all the questions; you could choose, for example, the 12 most common or relevant questions to the members of your group, and put them together in whatever combination you thought best.
- The course could also be run as a series of two or three Saturday morning seminars, doing 6 or 9 units at a time.

The video

To make it easier to know where you're up to on the video, each segment has a running title at the bottom of the screen, displaying which question is currently being discussed. To help you navigate, here is a list of the segments and there approximate start times on the video.

Segment	Start time (min:sec)
Introduction: How to answer questions	00:00
Q1. How do I know God exists in the first place?	08:03
Q2. Is the New Testament story about Jesus reliable?	12:02
Q3. Wasn't Jesus just another great religious teacher?	15:46
Q4. Did Jesus really come back from the dead?	17:34
Q5. Hasn't science disproved Christianity?	20:30
Q6. How do we account for all the suffering in the world?	24:03
Q7. Does 'faith' mean believing things we can't accept?	27:35
Q8. What about miracles — can miracles actually happen?	29:55
Q9. What about those people who have never heard about Jesus?	32:54
Q10. What about other religions; are they all true?	36:12
Q11. Aren't all people basically good?	38:54
Q12. Can we just be good enough to please God?	42:03
Q13. Do you have to go to church to be a Christian?	45:48
Q14. Could it be said that the Bible is sexist?	48:53
Q15. What does the Bible say about homosexuality?	52:34
Q16. Isn't Christianity responsible for a great deal of the environmental disaster in our world?	54:52
Q17. Aren't Christians just hypocrites?	57:10

Contributors

We're very grateful to those who so generously gave of their time in the filming of the video:

Kirsten Birkett is the editor of kategoria and the author of several well-known books including Unnatural Enemies: an introduction to Science and Christianity.

Peter Bolt is the head of the New Testament department at Moore Theological College, Sydney.

John Chapman is a well-known Bible-teacher and evangelist, and was for many years the Director of the Department of Evangelism in Sydney.

Kim Kemmis has degrees in theology, and early Christian and Jewish studies, and works with a ministry that helps people come out of homosexuality.

Ian Powell is the Rector of St Barnabas' Anglican Church, Broadway.

Kel Richards is a well-known broadcaster, Christian author and speaker.

Claire Smith is currently working on a PhD in New Testament history, and ministers with her husband Rob at Christ Church, St Ives.

Rob Smith has recently completed his Masters in Theology, and ministers at Christ Church, St Ives.

Our thanks, too, to Anglican Television, Sydney, for their help in the production process.

Our goal in producing this course has been to equip Christians to answer people's questions wisely, graciously and compellingly. Our hope and prayer is that as they do so, they will give glory to Christ by pointing people to him, and that in his time and through his grace, many more might come to know him as their Lord.

Simon Roberts and Tony Payne
March 2001

Introduction
How to answer questions

The importance of questions

There are two basic reasons why we need to know the answers to the various curly questions that are dealt with in this course.

For one thing, they can bother us as Christians. Is the New Testament really a reliable source of information? What about all the advances in science—don't they somehow render our belief in God old-fashioned? And why is there so much suffering in the world, if God is so loving? At one time or another, these sorts of questions have passed through our minds as Christian believers. And it is important that we know the answers to them. God is not afraid of the truth. By asking, researching and answering the questions that arise in our minds, we can only come to grasp his truth more fully.

Secondly, we of course need to know how to answer those who raise these questions with us. As both Peter and Paul remind us, to be able to answer graciously and gently when we are called upon to do so is an important part of every Christian's relationship with 'outsiders' (as Paul calls them in Colossians 4; see also 1 Peter 3:15-16). In fact, it is often the way we get into conversations with people about Christ and the gospel. As a question is raised—whether privately or around the lunch table at work—the way we react will either adorn the gospel and point towards Christ, or discredit Christ and reinforce people's prejudices against Christianity. It is important to be ready to answer well.

And so to this course. In this opening unit, we'll discuss some general principles about how to answer questions about the Christian faith, before moving on in the following units to work through the 17 most common questions asked about God and Christianity.

Think & discuss

1. Look through the list of common questions:

   a. Tick the ones that have bothered you at some stage:

   ☐ How do I know God exists in the first place?

   ☐ Is the New Testament story about Jesus reliable?

   ☐ Wasn't Jesus just another great religious teacher?

   ☐ Did Jesus really come back from the dead?

   ☐ Hasn't science disproved Christianity?

   ☐ How do we account for all the suffering in the world?

   ☐ Does 'faith' mean believing things we can't accept?

   ☐ What about miracles—can miracles actually happen?

   ☐ What about those people who have never heard about Jesus?

   ☐ What about other religions; are they all true?

   ☐ Aren't all people basically good?

   ☐ Can we just be good enough to please God?

   ☐ Do you have to go to church to be a Christian?

   ☐ Could it be said that the Bible is sexist?

   ☐ What does the Bible say about homosexuality?

   ☐ Isn't Christianity responsible for a great deal of the environmental disaster in our world?

   ☐ Aren't Christians just hypocrites?

   b. Which ones have you been asked by someone else? How would you rate the answer you gave?

2. What general principles do you think are important in answering questions? Jot down anything you can think of.

▦ Watch & write

Now play the introductory segment on the video, and take notes below. (NB. Throughout this course, space is provided for you to take notes during the video segments. We strongly recommend that you do take notes, not just so that you can easily refer back to the material, but to aid your listening and recall. Taking notes is 'active listening'—it is harder work than 'passive listening', but much more effective.)

Outline for notes:
1. Why it is important

2. What to do before answering

3. What to do while answering

4. What to do after answering

Pray

Conclude by praying about:
- the kind of person you need to be in order to answer questions well
- people you know, whose questions you may have to answer
- your own growth in knowledge and skills during this course

Question 1:
How do I know God exists in the first place?

Think & discuss

1. How would you go about answering this question? Jot down the kinds of things you think should be included in an answer.

2. If you are doing this course in a small group, briefly share the various points you came up with. Expand your list of possible ways to answer this question.

Watch & write

Before we play the first video answer, it is worth remembering that the answers recorded on the video are not the only answers, nor do they convey every point that could be made. They represent the main and important points to be made, and they do so in the individual style and wording of the presenters. You need to work out how you would convey the answer to this question in your own words and personal style. This is the purpose of the final step in each unit (see below) where you summarize your own answer to the question.

Outline for notes:

1. The argument from creation

2. The argument from human life and personality

3. The argument from Jesus

Summarize your answer

Write down in your own words, using three or four simple points, how you would answer the question: *How do I know God exists in the first place?*

Further reading:

John Chapman, *A Fresh Start* (Matthias Media), ch 6-8

Question 2:
Is the New Testament story about Jesus reliable?

Think & discuss

1. How would you go about answering this question? Jot down the kinds of things you think should be included in an answer.

2. If you are doing this course in a small group, briefly share the various points you came up with. Expand your list of possible ways to answer this question.

▦ Watch & write

Watch the video answer to question 2, and take notes in the space provided below.

Outline for notes

1. Intro: Why is this question important?

2. The New Testament

    a. As history

    b. Its relation to other historical information we know

    c. Its literary style

    d. The documents: no reason for scepticism

3. Conclusion

Summarize your answer

Write down in your own words, using three or four simple points, how you would answer the question: *Is the New Testament story about Jesus reliable?*

Further reading:
Paul Barnett, *Is the New Testament History?* (Paternoster)

Question 3:
Wasn't Jesus just another great religious teacher?

Think & discuss

1. How would you go about answering this question? Jot down the kinds of things you think should be included in an answer.

2. If you are doing this course in a small group, briefly share the various points you came up with. Expand your list of possible ways to answer this question.

Watch & write

Watch the video answer to question 3, and take notes in the space provided below.

Outline for notes

1. What was Jesus mission? What did he say about it? A twofold purpose:

    a.

    b.

2. This mission explains the kinds of things that Jesus did:

    -

    -

    -

    -

Summarize your answer

Write down in your own words, using three or four simple points, how you would answer the question: *Wasn't Jesus just another great religious teacher?*

Further reading?

Paul Barnett, The Truth about Jesus (Aquila Press)

Question 4:
Did Jesus really come back from the dead?

Think & discuss

1. How would you go about answering this question? Jot down the kinds of things you think should be included in an answer.

2. If you are doing this course in a small group, briefly share the various points you came up with. Expand your list of possible ways to answer this question.

▦ Watch & write

Watch the video answer to question 4, and take notes in the space provided below.

Outline for notes

1. Intro: a crucial question

2. Three things that need explaining:
   a. The empty tomb

   b. The appearances

   c. The birth and incredible growth of the Christian movement

3. Which explanation?

Summarize your answer

Write down in your own words, using three or four simple points, how you would answer the question: *Did Jesus really come back from the dead?*

Further reading:
Frank Morrison, *Who Moved the Stone?* (OM Publishing)
Peter Bolt, "Questing for Jesus" *kategoria* 8 (Matthias Media)

Question 5:
Hasn't science disproved Christianity?

Think & discuss

1. How would you go about answering this question? Jot down the kinds of things you think should be included in an answer.

2. If you are doing this course in a small group, briefly share the various points you came up with. Expand your list of possible ways to answer this question.

▐▐ Watch & write

Watch the video answer to question 5, and take notes in the space provided below.

Outline for notes

1. The usual argument
   a. Science replaces God

   b. But which God does this disprove?

2. The God of the Bible
   a. His relation to creation

   b. God's relation to science

Summarize your answer

Write down in your own words, using three or four simple points, how you would answer the question: *Hasn't science disproved Christianity?*

Further reading:

Kirsten Birkett, Unnatural Enemies: an introduction to Science and Christianity (Matthias Media)

Question 6:
How do we account for all the suffering in the world?

Think & discuss

1. How would you go about answering this question? Jot down the kinds of things you think should be included in an answer.

2. If you are doing this course in a small group, briefly share the various points you came up with. Expand your list of possible ways to answer this question.

▄▄ Watch & write

Watch the video answer to question 6, and take notes in the space provided below.

Outline for notes

1. Why is there suffering?
   a. Creation

   b. Fall

   c. Two consequences

2. Why doesn't God get rid of the evil and suffering?
   a. Careful: it might mean you

   b. He has set a day

   c. How he has dealt with evil and suffering

Summarize your answer

Write down in your own words, using three or four simple points, how you would answer the question: *How do we account for all the suffering in the world?*

Further reading:
D. A. Carson, *How Long, O Lord?* (Baker)

Question 7:
Does 'faith' mean believing things we can't accept?

Think & discuss

1. How would you go about answering this question? Jot down the kinds of things you think should be included in an answer.

2. If you are doing this course in a small group, briefly share the various points you came up with. Expand your list of possible ways to answer this question.

🎬 Watch & write

Watch the video answer to question 7, and take notes in the space provided below.

Outline for notes
1. Intro: the common view of faith

2. What is 'faith' in the Bible?
   a. 'faith' and 'belief'

   b. a matter of trust

   c. not a blind leap

3. Conclusion

Summarize your answer

Write down in your own words, using three or four simple points, how you would answer the question: *Does 'faith' mean believing things we can't accept?*

Further reading:
Paul E. Little, *How to give away your faith* (IVP) ch 6.

Question 8:
What about miracles—can miracles actually happen?

Think & discuss

1. How would you go about answering this question? Jot down the kinds of things you think should be included in an answer.

2. If you are doing this course in a small group, briefly share the various points you came up with. Expand your list of possible ways to answer this question.

Watch & write

Watch the video answer to question 8, and take notes in the space provided below.

Outline for notes

1. God makes everything happen
   a. In ordinary ways, and in extraordinary ways

   b. The 'laws of nature'

2. God can do as he wishes
   a. The sun standing still

   b. Using ordinary processes in extraordinary ways

Summarize your answer

Write down in your own words, using three or four simple points, how you would answer the question: *What about miracles—can miracles actually happen?*

Further reading:

Roger White, "Miracles and rational belief" *kategoria* 6 (Matthias Media)
Archie Poulos, "Miracles as Evidence for Christianity" *kategoria* 6 (Matthias Media)

Question 9:

What about those people who have never heard about Jesus?

Think & discuss

1. How would you go about answering this question? Jot down the kinds of things you think should be included in an answer.

2. If you are doing this course in a small group, briefly share the various points you came up with. Expand your list of possible ways to answer this question.

Watch & write

Watch the video answer to question 9, and take notes in the space provided below.

Outline for notes

1. The basis of judgement

2. What everyone knows

3. It's what you *do* with what you know

4. What about those who *have* heard?

Summarize your answer

Write down in your own words, using three or four simple points, how you would answer the question: *What about those people who have never heard about Jesus?*

Further reading:
Paul E. Little, *How to give away your faith* (IVP) ch 6

30

Question 10:
What about other religions: are they all true?

Think & discuss

1. How would you go about answering this question? Jot down the kinds of things you think should be included in an answer.

2. If you are doing this course in a small group, briefly share the various points you came up with. Expand your list of possible ways to answer this question.

Watch & write

Watch the video answer to question 10, and take notes in the space provided below.

Outline for notes

1. What did Jesus come to do?

    a.

    b.

2. Ignorance of other religions

3. Conclusion

Summarize your answer

Write down in your own words, using three or four simple points, how you would answer the question: *What about other religions; are they all true?*

Further reading:
Fritz Ridenour, *So what's the difference?* (Regal Books)

Question 11:
Aren't all people basically good?

Think & discuss

1. How would you go about answering this question? Jot down the kinds of things you think should be included in an answer.

2. If you are doing this course in a small group, briefly share the various points you came up with. Expand your list of possible ways to answer this question.

▥ Watch & write

Watch the video answer to question 11, and take notes in the space provided below.

Outline for notes

1. Bible says two things:
   a.

   b.

2. Our own little gods
   a. the consequences for our relationships

3. Conclusion

Summarize your answer

Write down in your own words, using three or four simple points, how you would answer the question: *Aren't all people basically good?*

Further reading:
John Chapman, *A Fresh Start* (Matthias Media), ch 11

34

Question 12:
Can we just be good enough to please God?

Think & discuss

1. How would you go about answering this question? Jot down the kinds of things you think should be included in an answer.

2. If you are doing this course in a small group, briefly share the various points you came up with. Expand your list of possible ways to answer this question.

🎬 Watch & write

Watch the video answer to question 12, and take notes in the space provided below.

Outline for notes

1. Intro: just because we give ourselves the thumbs up...

2. What does God expect of us?
   a. The second commandment

   b. The first commandment

   c. An illustration

3. Conclusion: we need Jesus

Summarize your answer

Write down in your own words, using three or four simple points, how you would answer the question: *Can we just be good enough to please God?*

Further reading:

John Chapman, *A Fresh Start* (Matthias Media), ch 11

Question 13:
Do you have to go to church to be a Christian?

Think & discuss

1. How would you go about answering this question? Jot down the kinds of things you think should be included in an answer.

2. If you are doing this course in a small group, briefly share the various points you came up with. Expand your list of possible ways to answer this question.

🎬 Watch & write

Watch the video answer to question 13, and take notes in the space provided below.

Outline for notes

1. No, if you…

2. Otherwise, yes
   a. Not about good and bad

   b. But forgiveness and following Jesus as Lord

   c. Netball not golf

3. Why church?
   a.

   b.

   c.

Summarize your answer

Write down in your own words, using three or four simple points, how you would answer the question: *Do you have to go to church to be a Christian?*

Question 14:
Could it be said that the Bible is sexist?

Think & discuss

1. How would you go about answering this question? Jot down the kinds of things you think should be included in an answer.

2. If you are doing this course in a small group, briefly share the various points you came up with. Expand your list of possible ways to answer this question.

Watch & write

Watch the video answer to question 14, and take notes in the space provided below.

Outline for notes

1. In one sense, yes

2. In another sense, no

   a. In what sense equal?

   b. Role of women in New Testament

3. Conclusion

Summarize your answer

Write down in your own words, using three or four simple points, how you would answer the question: *Could it be said that the Bible is sexist?*

Further reading:

Susan Foh, *Women and the Word of God* (Presbyterian & Reformed)

40

Question 15:
What does the Bible say about homosexuality?

Think & discuss

1. How would you go about answering this question? Jot down the kinds of things you think should be included in an answer.

2. If you are doing this course in a small group, briefly share the various points you came up with. Expand your list of possible ways to answer this question.

Watch & write

Watch the video answer to question 15, and take notes in the space provided below.

Outline for notes

1. What the Bible says is wrong

2. Why?
   a. Doesn't work

   b. The purpose of sex

   c. What else is therefore wrong

3. What the Bible doesn't say

4. Conclusion: Jesus

Summarize your answer

Write down in your own words, using three or four simple points, how you would answer the question: *What does the Bible say about homosexuality?*

Further reading:
Thomas Schmidt, *Straight and Narrow?* (IVP)

42

Question 16:
Isn't Christianity responsible for a great deal of the environmental disaster in our world?

Think & discuss

1. How would you go about answering this question? Jot down the kinds of things you think should be included in an answer.

2. If you are doing this course in a small group, briefly share the various points you came up with. Expand your list of possible ways to answer this question.

Watch & write

Watch the video answer to question 16, and take notes in the space provided below.

Outline for notes

1. Intro: the argument that was put forward

2. Why is it wrong?
   a. Non-Christian countries

   b. What the creation passages actually say

   c. The true Christian attitude to the environment

3. Conclusion: the real problem

Summarize your answer

Write down in your own words, using three or four simple points, how you would answer the question: *Isn't Christianity responsible for a great deal of the environmental disaster in our world?*

Further reading:
Don Clugson, "Even 'deep ecology' is not deep enough" *kategoria 6* (Matthias Media)

Question 17:
Aren't Christians just hypocrites?

Think & discuss

1. How would you go about answering this question? Jot down the kinds of things you think should be included in an answer.

2. If you are doing this course in a small group, briefly share the various points you came up with. Expand your list of possible ways to answer this question.

▶ Watch & write

Watch the video answer to question 17, and take notes in the space provided below.

Outline for notes

1. A harsh accusation

2. Yet we are hypocrites

3. Conclusion: the alcoholic's prayer

Summarize your answer

Write down in your own words, using three or four simple points, how you would answer the question: *Aren't Christians just hypocrites?*

Where to from here?

Well done! You now should be equipped to answer the common questions that people ask about Christianity. Even if you can't instantly recall how you would answer, say, Question 6 (Hasn't science disproved Christianity?), we hope that you can now see that answering such a question is well within your reach. We hope that you have gained a new confidence to discuss Christian things with your friends and family, and that God in his kindness will give you many opportunities to do so.

As Kel Richards noted in his introduction, answering questions is very often how we get into conversations with people about the gospel. Rarely does someone roll up and say, "Good Sir, what must I do to be saved?" And we do not always have the boldness or the opportunity simply to say to a friend, "Listen, how about I explain Christianity to you". But questions do arise, and if we are confident to answer them it can lead to sharing the very content of the gospel with people.

To that end, a very useful next step would be to learn how to explain the gospel itself simply and clearly. The Matthias Media training course 2 *Ways to Live: Know the gospel, share the gospel* is an excellent means of doing this. For more details, see the information at the back of this workbook, or visit the Matthias Media website (www.matthiasmedia.com.au). Sharpening up your ability to explain the gospel will only add to your confidence in talking to others about your faith.

May God give you his wisdom and courage as you do so.

2 Ways to Live: Know the gospel, share the gospel

2 *Ways* to *Live* is perhaps the resource Matthias Media is best known for. Over the past 15 years or so, thousands of Christians worldwide have learnt the simple six-point outline of the gospel that is the centrepiece of 2 *Ways* to *Live*. Having learnt it, they have also discovered how to adapt this outline to their own style of speech to be able to share the gospel with others.

Over the seven sessions of the 2 *Ways* to *Live* training course, trainees: learn the statements and drawings of the gospel outline, practice adapting it to their own style of speech, look at what the Bible says about sharing the gospel, learn the importance of prayer, and gain some practical experience in sharing the gospel.

One of the key benefits of 2 *Ways* to *Live* is that it assumes very little prior knowledge. In our increasingly post-modern, biblically illiterate world, 2 *Ways* to *Live* has proven to be a very effective means of communicating the gospel in a clear, jargon-free way.

To find out more, download the 2 *Ways* to *Live* information sheet (pdf format) from our website (www.matthiasmedia.com.au/2wtl).

To evaluate the material, purchase the Leader's Manual. It contains the 2 *Ways* to *Live* outline, the rationale for the course, leader's notes, plus a copy of the Trainee Workbook.